50 Adventures
in the

States

Written by KATE SIBER

Illustrated by LYDIA HILL

WIDE EYED EDITIONS

CONTENTS

ARE YOU READY FOR A BIG ADVENTURE?

This book is about to take you on a whirlwind tour of the United States, from the mountains of Maine to the beaches of California, the volcanoes of Hawaii to the forests of Virginia!

You don't need special skills or smarts to head out on an adventure, just a positive spirit and a readiness to try new things. Learn to climb up rocky pinnacles in Alabama, dig for beautiful crystals in Oklahoma, and collect your own wild plants for dinner in Oregon. If you have lots of energy, scramble through a slot canyon in Utah, climb a mountain in New Hampshire, or explore a glacier in Alaska. To cool off, glide down a natural stone waterslide in Pennsylvania!

The U.S.A. is full of wild places and great ways to explore them, but some of the coolest adventures are right in our biggest cities, from kayaking in Boston to birding in New York City. With an intrepid spirit, you can also have fun exploring your very own backyard and neighborhood parks, discovering the cool birds, mammals, and plants that live there. No foray is too small for a sense of discovery. What's stopping you? Set forth and explore the big, wide, outdoor world both near and far in the 50 states!

ALABAMA

Hot and sweaty? Join the club! The weather in Alabama is very warm and humid. In summer, temperatures reach the high 90s.

See those white spots all over the rock? Climbers often use chalk to dry out their hands for better grip.

Some of the earth is wearing away from so much use—it's called erosion. To be a good steward, make sure you stay on the main trails.

"Sandrock" is the name used by rock climbers for Cherokee Rock Village.

CLIMB GIANT BOULDERS

At Cherokee Rock Village, sandstone pinnacles soar out of a mountain like giant fingers. Swing up, down, and sideways, while clambering around this rocky playground with all of your limbs. Dotted with knobs, divots, and pockets, these cliffs are like a natural jungle gym. Climbers actually have a name for this funky sport: bouldering. Since you don't go very high, it doesn't require any ropes or special equipment. (Although some sticky rubber-soled shoes certainly help.) See if you can climb to the very top of one of the pinnacles to look over Weiss Lake and the valley far below!

Embrace your inner gecko! Slip on a pair of tight-fitting climbing shoes with sticky rubber so you can scale up walls with ease.

Consider yourself lucky if you see a black bear. These giant mammals patrol the woods looking for insects, plants, berries, and small animals to eat.

Want to go really high? Get a friend to "spot" you. If you slip, they will direct your fall so you land right side up.

Bouldering has its own rating system to let you know how hard a climb is. A V1 "problem" is pretty easy. A V10 is really hard.

A crash pad is a foam mat that helps cushion your fall. Most have straps and fold up so you can carry them around.

Hear that slithering through the dry leaf litter? It might be a timber rattlesnake, which can grow to six feet. Don't worry, they usually steer clear of humans!

Alaska

WALK ON A GLACIER

Pull on your ice cleats and strap on your helmet—you're going on an adventure on the Matanuska Glacier! Scale icy slopes as you *crunch crunch* along the hard snow. Peer into ice caves painted a million shades of blue, and peek into deep spooky cracks known as crevasses. At the terminus, touch 600-year-old ice! From a distance, the glacier looks like a big block, but it's actually moving very, very slowly down the valley, steamrolling everything in its path. In winter, the glacier groans and pops as it builds and moves. And in summer, waterfalls rush and ice shards tinkle as it all melts in the sun.

Did you know that glacial ice covers 10 percent of all land area on Earth? That's 5.8 million square miles of glaciers and ice caps and sheets.

Sometimes the glacier looks like a zebra with its black lines. These are called debris bands.

Some of the glacial ice forms pointy blocks, called seracs. They are named after a type of Swiss cheese that also crumbles into blocky shapes.

Coyotes, wolves, moose, and bears live in the spruce and deciduous forests that surround the glacier.

Why is some ice white, and some blue? Blue ice has larger crystals and fewer air bubbles. When light passes through this dense ice, all of the colors in the spectrum are absorbed except blue, which is reflected back to our eyes.

Moraines are giant piles of dirt, rocks, and debris created and deposited by the glacier as it cuts into the mountains.

When encased in ice, glacier moss can survive for 1,500 years in a hibernation-like state called cryptobiosis.

In 1864, Colonel Kit Carson forced the Navajo out of the canyon. Many died on the "Long Walk" to Fort Sumter in New Mexico. Three years later, they returned after signing a treaty, but they had lost much of their homeland as well as their farms and sheep. Over years, they were able to rebuild.

From overlook points along the canyon's rim, gaze over amazing panoramic views.

Hogans are traditional Navajo homes. Some are cone-shaped, hogans are round, some and some have several sides. Navajo also live in different kinds of homes too.

Rock art comes in various forms. You might see petroglyphs, which are etched into the stone, or pictographs, which are painted onto the rock.

At the edge of the canyon's rim is a vertical line of divots in the rock. Those are hand- and toeholds that ancient people used to climb it.

ARIZONA

Yá'át'ééh! The Navajo use this word as a positive greeting. It loosely translates to "all is well" or "everything is good."

Spider Rock is an 800-foot pinnacle deep in the canyon. It is considered a sacred place.

Ravens are big, black, intelligent birds that loop overhead. They are one of the few species that saves items to use as tools later.

HORSEBACK RIDE WITH A NAVAJO GUIDE

As you trot on horseback through Canyon de Chelly, feel the sun on your face and the breeze through your hair. This is the land of the Diné, or Navajo people. For nearly 5,000 years, human beings have lived in and traveled through this canyon. You can still see rock art made by nomads and palaces built by ancestral Puebloan people between 1000 and 1300 C.E. The Navajo arrived in the 1700s. Today, visitors come from all over to see the magnificent sandstone canyon, which is protected as a national monument. Some Navajo families also still live on the valley floor tending sheep, orchards, and farms.

Mountain lions patrol the canyon at dusk and dawn but they are very secretive. It's unlikely you'd see one, but look for their tracks.

According to Diné legend, Spider Rock is the home of Spider Woman, who gave the people the gift of weaving.

ARKANSAS

Pawpaw trees grow deep in the forest. Their fruit looks like a pear and tastes like a cross between a mango and a banana.

Keep your eyes out for wildlife! Several herds of Rocky Mountain elk live near the river. Great blue herons and bald eagles soar overhead.

River otters have water-repellent fur and webbed feet for swimming. They can hold their breath for eight minutes.

Red-eared sliders like to sun themselves on logs in the river. See if you can pass by silently without all of them diving into the water.

KAYAK A WILD AND WINDING RIVER

Floating down the Buffalo National River in a kayak, dip your paddle into the blue-green water and listen to the sounds of water rippling. Along the banks, bluffs of sandstone, limestone, and dolomite rise as high as 590 feet. This waterway winds 135 miles from its headwaters through the Ozark Mountains and is one of the only undammed rivers left in the continental United States. Along the way, fish for smallmouth bass, swim in turquoise pools, and float through tunnels of leafy trees. Stop to explore an early 20th-century cabin or hike to waterfalls for a shower in their spray!

More than 100 different species of trees and shrubs live in the river corridor. Oak-hickory forests are most common.

Wild hogs are an invasive species. Listen for groups of them snorting and crashing through the forest and smell their musky scent.

At least 59 species of fish live in the Buffalo River. If you're lucky, you might see a rainbow darter, a rare native fish.

The Buffalo River was once a popular seasonal hunting ground for the Osage people, who lived in what's now the southern Missouri area.

Some of the upper sections of the river have challenging whitewater rapids. The middle and lower sections feature flat water good for beginners.

Underneath all of the greenery, the ground looks like holey Swiss cheese. This karst geology creates lots of sinkholes, springs, and seeps. The area also has about 500 caves.

California

The most important part of this sport is choosing where to surf. Beginners should always try an easy break on a day with mellow waves.

If you see a dorsal fin, don't worry! It's probably a pod of passing dolphins.

Not ready to try surfing with a board? You can ride waves with just your body—no skills required! Just be sure to steer clear of whizzing surfboards.

Do you ride regular or goofy foot? Goofy foot means you have your right leg forward.

The Pacific is cold! Water temperatures at Venice Beach hover in the high 60s.

Venice Beach is a hive of activity— and a hoot! Walk or bike to see people in costume, street performers, artists, fortune tellers, and visitors from around the world.

Longboards, bodyboards, and soft-top surfboards are good choices for newbies. Later, you can try a shorter board that turns more easily.

Surfing doesn't need a lot of equipment, just a surfboard, a leash that attaches to your ankle, and a wetsuit. (Or in warmer climates, a rash guard or swimsuit.)

Keep a lookout for stingrays, which have barb-like tails. They like to hang out on the seafloor. When wading out, shuffle along to avoid stepping on one.

A thin coating of wax keeps your board sticky so you don't slip.

SURF VENICE BEACH

Surf's up at Venice Beach! On the coast of L.A., artists, performers and muscle-bound fitness buffs crowd the beach. But being a surfer is the most fun of all. Surfing may have been born in Hawaii but it grew popular right here in southern California. Pull on your wetsuit, grab your board, and paddle out! The wind is mellow and the waves are glassy. Beyond the breakers, it's peaceful among the fish and the dolphins. You'll have to paddle hard to catch a wave. Pop up to standing and feel the power of the ocean speed you along. It feels like flying!

The Ouray Ice Park makes the ice by spraying the steep walls with water. The walls naturally freeze in the low temperatures.

At the Ouray Ice Park, you can walk right up to the kids' wall, but other areas require you to rappel in from the top.

CLIMB A FROZEN WATERFALL

Thwack! Thwack! That's the sound of your ice axes hitting a frozen waterfall. With spiky metal crampons on your feet, you're scaling a vertical sheet of ice like a superhero! The Ouray Ice Park is a magical kingdom of frosty cascades tucked in a narrow canyon. Ice climbers come from all over the world to clamber up these frozen falls. At a special area for kids, children as young as seven try 40-foot-tall routes. Make sure you have your harness, rope, and a helmet on your head. Then take a deep breath of chilly mountain air and scamper your way up a slippery curtain of ice!

Ice climbers say that the sport is like a dance. Start to feel the rhythm with each thwack of your axe and chink of your crampons.

Not many animals live in the ice park itself. But in the mountains beyond, look for bighorn sheep.

"On belay?" When a climber is tied to the rope and ready to climb, she asks her belayer if she's on belay. "Belay on," "Climbing," "Climb on."

As you climb, the person on the ground who holds the rope (with a special device) is called a belayer.

COLORADO

In the town of Ouray, hot springs bubble up out of the ground. After climbing, take a dip in one of the steamy pools.

Forests line the edge of the gorge and dot the cliffs beyond. Two common species are white fir and ponderosa pine.

What's a crampon? It's a metal plate with spikes that attaches to a boot. Crampons allow climbers to gain traction on slippery surfaces.

Practice good etiquette by avoiding the tracks that cross-country skiers like to use. It's more fun to go off trail anyway!

Beavers are lively all winter. Near the beaver pond, discover their telltale signs, including holes in the ice and chew-marks on trees.

If you're going down a steep hill, bend your knees and keep your weight back so you don't somersault down the slope!

Poles aren't necessary but they can help you keep your balance. Make sure to get ones with snow baskets.

SNOWSHOE THROUGH FORESTS AND MEADOWS

Big fat snowflakes are falling as you tramp through snowy meadows and forests with snowshoes on your feet. Welcome to Northwest Park in Windsor, Connecticut, a giant reserve that's ripe for exploration! The snow sparkles and everything is quiet. Listen for the sounds of trees creaking in the breeze and look for the tracks of deer and foxes that silently wander the wintry land. If you're a beginner, you can start by following the tracks of others. But then, let your imagination go wild. With snowshoes on your feet, you can go up, down, and around. Explore the deep woods and go anywhere you like!

Stop and listen—snow dampens sound and makes everything peaceful and quiet.

CONNECTICUT

Catch a glimpse of the shy white-tailed deer looking for twigs, leaves, and other deer food. Only the male deer, the bucks, have antlers.

See that flash out of the corner of your eye? Red foxes are quick and resourceful, eating lots of different types of food. They also have good hearing so they can listen to prey scurrying about.

Starting around mid-February, you might see a spile (tap) and a bucket attached to a maple tree. New Englanders collect sap to make into maple syrup for your pancakes.

Along the way, look for wildlife tracks in the snow. Some snowshoers have even spotted feather prints from owls hunting the night before.

Delaware

Dolphins are one of the few animal species that like to play. Watch as they frolic in your boat's bow wake.

Delaware Bay is chock full of marine life because it's a mid-Atlantic border area where southern and northern species mix.

To find prey, dolphins make clicking sounds then listen for the echoes after they bounce off nearby objects.

Dolphins chow on live fish like menhaden and blue fish. To us they seem smelly and oily, but dolphins find them delectable.

Humpback whales and dolphins like to eat the same kinds of fish, so they often hang out together. See if you can also spot a rare North Atlantic right whale!

Atlantic bottlenose dolphins are the most common species but lots of others live here too. Look for striped, white-sided, and Risso's dolphins.

Several species of sea turtles visit the bay and ocean coast. The largest are leatherbacks, which eat jellyfish and weigh up to one ton, almost as much as a small car.

Did you know that sharks are actually scared of dolphins? Coastal bottlenose dolphins grow to 750 pounds and will ram sharks in the gills. Ouch!

The salt marshes are important nurseries where fish grow up before going out to sea to get eaten by bigger fish.

Calves have to learn how to leap out of the water. Their tails are all wiggly, just like humans are wobbly when they learn to walk.

Plastic trash often makes its way to the ocean and that's bad news for marine creatures. You can help by using less plastic, reusing, recycling, and cutting your six-pack rings. Or start a beach clean-up!

SEE DOLPHINS FROLIC

Out on the water in Delaware Bay, fishing boats zoom around and a salty wind blows. This estuary is full of activity, especially underwater! The stars of the show are Atlantic bottlenose dolphins, which cruise around in small families. When they're getting ready to go south, you might see pods as big as 70 or 80. Dolphins aren't shy at all and come right up to your boat—sometimes so close you can nearly touch them! With eyes on the sides of their heads, they roll over to take a look at you. Lots of other marine creatures live here too—look for whales, sharks, and sea turtles.

The Florida Reef Tract, which stretches along the southeast coast of the state, is the largest living coral reef system in the United States.

Five sea turtle species swim in Florida's waters. The loggerhead is most common. With its strong jaws, it crushes crabs, clams, and other food.

At night, parrotfish make themselves cocoons out of mucus to sleep in. The covering helps protect them from predators. Can you imagine dozing in a sleeping bag of snot?

SNORKEL A RAINBOW REEF

Off the Florida Keys, a wild underwater world awaits just below the surface of the sea. Put on your mask, snorkel, and fins and jump in! Coral reefs are like giant cities and they're full of activity both day and night. Colorful critters like angelfish, damselfish, and butterflyfish dart about. Moray eels hide in crevices and flash their teeth. Gorgonian sea fans sway back and forth in the swells. Look for a cleaning station, where tiny shrimp, wrasses, and gobies give big fish a cleaning like a car wash. Don't forget to look out into the deep blue—you might glimpse a reef shark or a sea turtle passing by.

Bluehead wrasses are small fish that are all born female. Some of them develop into boys over the course of their lives.

Corals are actually tiny animals that create skeletons of calcium carbonate, or limestone. Their skeletons are hard as rock, and over time they create giant reefs.

Spotted eagle rays soar through shallow water near coral reefs. They can grow up to 7.5 feet wide.

Hard corals come in all sorts of cool shapes and sizes. Find species that look like stars, plates, brains, and even elk antlers!

FLORIDA

Corals live symbiotically with tiny algae called zooxanthellae and come in all sorts of wacky hues.

Nurse sharks are pretty mellow by shark standards. They are bottom-dwellers, so you might see one resting on the sea floor.

Barracuda are attracted to shiny objects because they often prey on silvery fish, so leave your watch and jewelry at home!

In the 1800s, mills along the river used water power to make paper, wool, cotton, and other goods. You can still see some of the stone and timber ruins.

PADDLE WHITEWATER ON THE CHATTAHOOCHEE RIVER

The sound of rushing water grows louder and louder as you near a whitewater rapid in your sturdy raft. Hold on to your paddle as you bounce through the roiling waves! On a sweltering summer day, join the party as a flotilla of Atlanta locals cruises down the river in kayaks, rafts, canoes, and inflatable tubes. In between long calm sections, the Chattahoochee River is a splashy rollercoaster with its easy Class I and II rapids. In a quiet moment, spot some of the river's amazing wildlife—an osprey looping lazily overhead, trout circling beneath your boat, or a river otter frolicking in the shallows.

The banks of the river are home to lots of overhanging rocks. People have used these areas as shelters for as long as 10,000 years.

Zip up your life jacket! This key piece of equipment keeps you afloat if you fall out of your craft.

A giant prehistoric-looking bird flaps over the river. It's a great blue heron with a five-foot wingspan.

The river remains a chilly 50 degrees year-round because the water is released from the bottom of a lake through a dam.

Trout, bass, and catfish ply these waters along with 20 other species of fish. With a fishing rod, see if you can catch one.

Ribbit, ribbit. The Chattahoochee River National Recreation Area is full of frogs and toads. Listen for their evening symphony.

Diving Rock towers more than 20 feet above the river. If you're a strong swimmer and are feeling brave, jump off feet first and rocket into the water.

Before European colonization, the Creek lived on the south bank of the river and the Cherokee lived on the north side.

Some locals call the river the "Hooch" for short. The river threads through the outskirts of Atlanta, the biggest city in the state.

A curious duck wants to say hi to you. Pick out which ducks are the male mallards—they have green heads and yellow bills.

Hawaii

The Hawaiian archipelago is located 2,000 miles from the nearest continent. It's one of the most isolated island chains in the world.

When measured from the bottom of the sea, Mauna Loa is the biggest mountain on Earth by volume. Its bulk takes up nearly 20,000 cubic miles of space.

Kīlauea erupted dramatically in 2018, and the volcano's summit collapsed. The lava flows destroyed more than 700 homes, and thousands of earthquakes transformed the landscape.

EXPLORE AN ACTIVE VOLCANO

On the Big Island of Hawaii, behold the fiery glow of live lava! The hot goo oozes in rivers and spurts in fountains all the way down to the sea. When it hits the cool water, it hardens into stone and giant plumes of steam rise up into the sky. Hawai'i Volcanoes National Park is home to two of the most active volcanoes on Earth: Kīlauea and Mauna Loa. Sometimes the volcanoes take a break from erupting, but there are always amazing things to explore, like cave-like lava tubes and fumaroles where gases swirl up from deep in the ground.

Pele is the Hawaiian goddess of fire. Legend holds that she lives in Kīlauea's Halema'uma'u Crater. Hawaiians leave offerings, sing songs, and hula dance to honor her. Some say they can see her profile in flowing lava.

Before colonization, Native Hawaiians once made capes out of the orange-red feathers of 'I'iwi birds. The garments were a symbol of power and status.

The 'Apapane is a red honeycreeper that loves to feast on the nectar of 'ōhi'a flowers. Spot it in high-altitude forests.

The 'ōhi'a is the most common native tree. It is often the first to sprout out of a newly hardened lava flow.

More than 1,600 years ago, the Polynesians arrived on the islands. To get here, they bravely traveled more than 2,400 miles across the ocean in giant canoes.

About 70 million years ago, plants and animals started to grow on these bare rocky islands. More than 90 percent of the native species are endemic, which means they live nowhere else on Earth.

This park has seven different life zones, from the steamy coast to the barren alpine areas near Mauna Loa's peak. The temperature can drop 15 degrees from sea to summit.

SOAK IN WILD HOT SPRINGS

Have you ever been outside on a cool spring day wearing only your swimsuit? Well, this is the occasion! Slip into a steamy natural hot springs pool and stare up at the cool blue sky. Idaho has about 130 soak-able hot springs, the most of any state. Some require a big hike, but at Kirkham, all you have to do is walk down a steep trail. The water simmers up from deep in the earth and rolls down the hillside. It collects in pools by the bank of the South Fork of the Payette River. Some of the hot water even launches off cliffs in steaming waterfalls. Take a warm shower heated by the earth itself!

A huge bird swoops down to the river! It's a bald eagle looking for fish to eat.

Hot springs abound in Idaho because of a large fault system. These cracks in the earth allow groundwater to trickle thousands of feet deep, where it warms up and returns to the surface piping hot.

One local resident is a plump rodent the size of a house cat that likes to whistle. Idahoans call these groundhogs "whistle pigs."

In the summer, rafters and kayakers paddle through whitewater rapids right near the springs.

In the summer, the springs are full of lots of friendly people. In winter, you can have this all-natural spa to yourself.

How hot do you like your bath? There are different pools with water temperatures that range from just warm to piping hot.

The ancestors of the Nez Perce, Shoshone-Paiute, and Shoshone-Bannock tribes all used this land before Euro-American colonization. The hot springs were and still are spiritually important to them.

Kirkham Hot Springs is surrounded by ponderosa pines, which are adapted to wildfire. Their height and thick bark help them withstand fires.

Sniffing the moist air, you might wonder: What's that faint egg smell? That's sulfur, a naturally occurring gas that is often released at hot springs.

The heat of the springs actually makes you sweat. Be sure to guzzle down plenty of water.

ICE SKATE IN CHICAGO

Layer up and lace up your skates. It's wintertime in Chicago and the whole city is frosty and white. That means it's time to glide across the ice on the city's famous skating ribbon! Unlike boring old oval rinks, this one winds like a snake and is twice as long as a normal rink. Bend your knees—it might take practice. But pretty soon you'll be soaring along like a pro. Float and twirl among families, figure skaters, athletes, and canoodling couples. Once you've got your balance, don't forget to look up. You're surrounded by some of the most gigantic skyscrapers in the windy city!

Brrrr! Gusts of wind blast off Lake Michigan. The lake water steadies the temperature, but if it freezes, those breezes are burly!

Chicago's famous skyscrapers loom above you. Can you pick out the Prudential, Aon Center, and Smurfit-Stone buildings?

Maggie Daley Park also has a playground with three-story slides. In the winter, the steel is cold, which makes them crazy fast! (Even adults like to play on them.)

Clear the rink! A Zamboni is a big machine that resurfaces the ice, making it smooth again after all the skate marks. It was invented in the 1940s.

Tuckered out? Hot chocolate is on the way.

The skating ribbon is next to Lake Michigan. Did you know that the city of Chicago has 26 miles of lakeshore and 25 beaches?

In the summer, after the ice melts, inline skaters and skateboarders cruise on the ribbon's dry pavement.

On cold winter days, long underwear and hats will make you really toasty and happy.

Chicago is the third largest city in the U.S. and has about 2.7 million residents.

ILLINOIS

Regular fishing in a lake, pond, or reservoir is called spin cast or closed face fishing.

Anglers love fishing for different reasons. It's exciting to catch one, fun to spend time with your family, and peaceful and relaxing to wait for a bite.

For tackle (fishing-speak for equipment) you'll need a push-button rod and reel. A weight or "sinker" keeps the baited hook under the surface.

A bobber floats at the top. If it bobs, you know a fish is munching.

To trick the fish into biting your hook, you need bait. Worms, larvae, grasshoppers, crickets, even a chunk of bread or hot dog will do.

CATCH YOUR OWN DINNER

Sitting at the end of a dock with a fishing rod, look behind you then cast your line into the lake. Watch carefully . . . The line goes taut. You've got a bite! "Fish on!" you say. Reel in your fish and see what it is. It might be a bluegill, which grow up to a foot long and are easy to find in Indiana's plentiful lakes, streams, and reservoirs. Once you've caught your fish, you can either carefully take the hook out and let it swim away, or fillet it and take it home for a tasty fresh-caught dinner.

Indiana has tons of water, which means the state also has tons of fish, such as black bass, smallmouth bass, largemouth bass, and catfish.

A blaze of color appears out of the cattails. It's a beautiful red-winged blackbird taking off from its nest.

Indiana

A huge bug with gossamer wings buzzes by. Dragonflies are nimble fliers and generally eat their meals (insects) mid-air.

From the city to the countryside, fish are right under your nose! Look for them anywhere from Delaware Lake in Indianapolis to Worster Lake near South Bend.

A muskrat splashes about in the shallows. This small water-loving mammal has big feet for swimming. It builds little houses that resemble haystacks.

Anglers love bluegill. These swimmers are active much of the day and have delicious white, flaky fillets.

BIKE ACROSS THE STATE

With more than 10,000 other cyclists, zoom along on a ribbon of blacktop through the heartland of America. RAGBRAI is a giant group bicycle ride that has traveled from the western border to the eastern border of Iowa every July since 1973. Pedal through huge cornfields, pastures, forests, river valleys, and tiny little farm towns, but beware, this place is hillier than it looks! Farmhouses and siloes dot the land, tractors put-put along, and pigs, cows, horses, and chickens roam the fields. The ride is a big, fun party and over the course of a week, you'll surely make new friends. Don't leave Iowa without a yummy slice of homemade pie—or maybe a few!

For at least 11,000 years, humans have lived in what is now known as Iowa. These people included the Oneota culture, the Ioway, the Sioux, and later, the Sauk, Meskwaki, Potawatomi, and Winnebago.

RAGBRAI stands for the Register's Annual Great Bicycle Ride Across Iowa. The ride is organized by The Des Moines Register, a newspaper.

You'll want a helmet and gloves to protect your noggin and paws. A mirror, mounted on your bike or helmet, is also helpful to see what's behind you.

With so many riders, safety is key. Remember to stop slowly and pull off to the side so that others don't run into you.

Iowa

Cyclists take their time on this non-competitive ride. Stop to play games, listen to music, or watch street performers. The person who has the most fun wins!

Did you know that RAGBRAI is the largest, longest, and oldest non-competitive bicycle tour in the world?

A SAG wagon is a funny name for a vehicle that picks up cyclists who are too tired to keep riding. To be picked up, stand on the side of the road with your bike turned upside down.

If you're not big enough to pedal a long way, you might be able to persuade your parents to pull you in a bike trailer!

In the evening, pitch your tent and hit the hay in a huge makeshift campground full of fellow cyclists.

RABGRAI cyclists can get a little silly. Join in the fun by wearing a costume or decorating your helmet with stuffed animals, sequins, feathers, and trinkets.

35

Tallgrass Prairie National Preserve is the only park in the country that protects the rare tallgrass prairie.

Did you know that prairies grow in places that are too dry for forests and too wet for deserts?

At the beginning of the 19th century, between 30 and 60 million bison roamed the plains. A century later, fewer than 1,000 remained. Thankfully, some people cared enough to save them from extinction. Now there are nearly 500,000. Most live on ranches and farms.

Grazing animals, such as bison and deer, help the prairie remain healthy. Their munching stimulates the plants to grow, and their hoofs till the soil, creating new places for seeds to sprout.

HIKE THROUGH TALLGRASS PRAIRIE

In the middle of the tallgrass prairie, low hills covered in wild grasses stretch as far as you can see. In fall, the plants are taller than you! At one time, these grasslands covered 170 million acres in the middle of the country, stretching from Canada to Texas. But in the 19th century, almost all of it was plowed to make way for farms and houses. Luckily, the remaining swaths are protected in the Flint Hills of Kansas. As you stroll along a dirt path, listen to the sashaying of grass in the breeze, gaze at the huge blue sky overhead, and look for bison and deer roaming in the distance.

The grasses are tallest in the fall when they reach heights of up to six feet. September and October are the best months to see tall grass.

KANSAS

Fire is a natural part of this landscape. It breaks down dead plants into ash and allows new plants room to grow.

Prairie plants are tough. They withstand heat, cold, wind, and fire. It helps that most of each plant is underground—some roots can grow 15 feet deep!

Humans have lived here for at least 12,000 years. Most recently, the Kansa, Kitikiti'sh (Wichita), Osage, and Pawnee all lived or hunted here. The state is named after the Kansa.

The Flint Hills are full of chert, also known as flint, which human beings used to make knives, tools, and art for thousands of years.

When mating, a male greater prairie chicken makes a spooky moaning noise. He raises his feathers, stamps his feet, and blows up air sacs on his neck to impress a lady.

These prairies contain some 70 different species of grass and more than 400 species of wildflower.

Jackrabbits, cottontails, rodents, lizards, and deer all live on the prairie. In forested areas near streams, foxes and bobcats prowl.

LEARN TO ROCK CLIMB

If you have ever dreamed of scampering up vertical walls like Spiderman, now is your chance. The Red River Gorge in eastern Kentucky has plenty of funky sandstone cliffs with more than 1,600 rock climbs. Pull on a pair of sticky-soled climbing shoes, don your harness, tie into a rope, then head skyward. Climbing is mental exercise as much as physical —let your imagination lead the way. To get up a route, you might have to crimp a tiny crack or pull on an outcropping, or even mantle up a ledge like you're getting out of a swimming pool. It's like vertical gymnastics!

Rock climbs sometimes have silly names, like "Belly of the Beast" or "Crack Attack" or "Gettin' Lucky in Kentucky."

Ancient people, Shawnee, Cherokee, and early homesteaders used some of the cliffs as shelters. If you find a spear point or a fragment of pottery, be sure to leave it where you found it so others can have fun discovering it too!

Thick, leafy deciduous forests cover the gorge. There are dozens of tree species—so many it's hard for foresters to keep track!

The gorge has hundreds of caves, which means it also has bats. Ten species, to be exact. Some bats eat more than half their weight in insects each night.

The Red River Gorge has more than 100 natural sandstone arches, each formed by wind, water, and erosion. There are also dozens of windows, which are baby arches that are still growing.

KENTUCKY

The toughest move
or series of moves
on a climb is called
the "crux."

Don't forget
your chalk
bag—a little bit
of chalk dries
out sweaty
hands so you
don't slip.

Climbers have a system for
grading routes. 5.2 is really
easy and 5.14 is really hard.
Only a few people in the
world can climb 5.14.

If you get tired, yell "take!" to your
belayer, the person holding the rope on
the ground. They'll pull up the slack
so you can hang and rest.

Climbers have funny names for
holds. A big jug is a huge pocket
or knob on the rock that is easy to
grab. A crimper is a teeny tiny hold.

GO SHRIMPING IN THE BAYOUS

From the shore of a peaceful bayou deep in southern Louisiana, toss your cast net into the drink. Pull in your line, dump the contents of your net into a big bucket, and see what you've got . . . dozens of shrimp are flopping about! These crustaceans love marshy habitats. As scavengers, they eat just about anything, including decaying plants and animals that they find on the bottom of the bayou or bay. For centuries, human beings have been collecting these protein-rich critters to eat. What classic Louisiana dish will you make out of your catch? How about some tasty shrimp po'boys, shrimp étoufée, shrimp creole, or seafood gumbo?

Big, graceful birds wade into the shallows. Great egrets, snowy egrets, green herons, and black-crowned night herons are just a few of the glamorous residents.

Commercial fishers use specialized nets to skim the bottom of the bayou for shrimp. Special devices help fish and sea turtles escape the net.

Shrimp spawn in the ocean then the tide carries larvae to shore. They grow up in interior marshes, then travel out to sea to start the cycle again.

The trickiest part of learning to cast net for shrimp is the toss itself. Practice slinging your net so it lands on the water fully unfurled and not folded or tangled.

With buck teeth and webbed toes, the nutria is pretty funny-looking. This invasive rodent is native to South America but now inhabits Louisiana marshes after some individuals escaped from fur farms in the 1930s.

Depending on the season, you can take between 50 and 100 pounds of shrimp from public waters in Louisiana. Hope you're hungry!

A bayou is a marshy outlet of a river, lake, or other body of water. Bayous can be either salty or freshwater.

Is that a log or an alligator? In these areas, male alligators can grow over 10 feet long.

White and brown shrimp are the most common species. They both have five sets of walking legs and five sets of swimming legs.

Shrimp are short-lived creatures. They usually don't live for much longer than 18 months.

LOUISIANA

Maine is nicknamed the Pine Tree State and it's not hard to see why. Also look for beautiful white birches on the side of ski runs.

Aprés-ski is a French term for what you do after skiing. And what do you do? Get a hot cocoa, of course!

Did you know that more than 90 percent of Maine is forested? That's the highest percentage of any state.

HIT THE SLOPES ON SKIS OR A BOARD

The air is nippy and the snow is deep. Pull on your goggles, click into your bindings, and push off—you're whizzing down a snowy Maine mountain as fast as a breeze! If you're just learning to ski or snowboard, be prepared for a tumble or two. Luckily the snow is soft (and so are you). Try out different kinds of trails—smooth groomers, bumpy moguls, and glades with loosely spaced trees. Once you have your ski or snowboard legs, venture into the terrain park. Try spinning and flipping on rails, pipes, and jumps. The air is just as fun as the snow!

If your legs get tired, try sledding on a snow tube—a giant inflatable rubber mattress.

What kind of trail is right for you? A green circle means it's the easiest way down. A blue square is intermediate, a black diamond is difficult, and a double black diamond is really difficult.

Richard's Run

Peterson Peak

Andrew's Summit Slope

Beginners sometimes turn their skis into a wedge shape, called a snowplow, so they can head down the mountain slowly.

Maine

Enjoy the views as the lift carries you up the peak.

A lift or a gondola whisks you to the top of the mountain. Some areas also have old rope tows—hold on to the rope and it'll pull you up the hill.

On closed courses, Olympic racers can reach speeds of up to 80 terrifying miles per hour. You won't reach these speeds, but you may feel like an Olympian!

Skiers call wide meandering trails cruisers. That's because you can sail all the way down with the breeze wafting through your hair!

If you prefer mellower terrain, cross-country skiing is for you. Taking big strides, you can gracefully glide across meadows and valleys.

PEDAL THE C&O CANAL TOWPATH

The C&O Canal Towpath starts in busy Washington, D.C. but in a matter of miles, it leads into forests full of wild wonders! Long ago, mule trains used to walk this path, straining against ropes that pulled boats through the canal. Now, cyclists, hikers, and runners zoom through the leafy forests and along beautiful cliffs. Some even ride the entire 184.5 miles all the way from Georgetown in the national capital to Cumberland, Maryland. Keep an eye out for critters such as deer, fox, bunnies, and eagles. And stop in Great Falls to take a ride on a real-life canal boat still pulled by mules!

Hear that staccato drumming? That's the sound of a downy woodpecker drilling a tree to slurp up insects with its long tongue.

Giant black birds with red heads circle overhead. Turkey vultures are scavengers, which means they like to eat animals that are already dead.

Completed in 1850, this famous canal connected the coalfields of the Allegheny Mountains to the coast. Imagine boats piled high with heaps of coal, wheat, and lumber.

In the summer, sniff the air and take in the sweet scent of blooming honeysuckle.

If you see a little hole in a tree, chances are something lives inside. It could be an opossum, the continent's only marsupial. They carry their babies in a tummy pouch.

In the old days, lock keepers let boats pass through the locks at all times of day or night.

Lock keepers lived in lockhouses. Some of these cabins have been restored to how they looked decades ago, and you can sleep in them overnight.

Since the canal closed down in 1924, plants have taken over. Now, the wetlands and forests are like sponges and help absorb floods and filter water.

A little droplet of luscious red peeks out from the greenery—a wild strawberry. These berries are important sweet treats for wildlife.

Back when the canal was working, whole families would operate the boats, including the kids. Most didn't go to school except in winter when the canal was closed. Can you imagine being in charge of a bunch of mules?

Maryland

On shore, the Boston Pops orchestra plays tunes such as the "1812 Overture" while the army sets off cannons.

Can you pick out the (new) John Hancock Tower from the Boston skyline? The tallest building in all of New England, it stands 62 stories high.

The old John Hancock building flashes lights depending on the weather. Just remember this poem: "Steady blue, clear view. Flashing blue, clouds due. Steady red, rain ahead. Flashing red, snow instead."

This city is famous for its history, such as the Boston Tea Party, when colonists angry about unfair taxes tossed tons of British tea into the harbor in 1773. It was one of the events that led to the American Revolution.

FLOAT THE CHARLES RIVER ON THE FOURTH OF JULY

BOOM! KAPOW! Red, white, and blue fireworks are bursting overhead! It's the Fourth of July and the city of Boston has one of the largest, oldest, and best celebrations in the country. The greatest seat of all is in a canoe or kayak in the middle of the Charles River, where the pyrotechnics shoot up from a barge. Paddle out among all of the other crafts and vessels, both big and small. Gaze up at the night sky, feel the thundering of the fireworks in your bones, and bask in the otherworldly glow reflected in the water. Happy birthday, America!

With all of the hustle and bustle on July 4, the animals are probably hiding. But on a regular day you might see beavers, muskrats, ducks, geese, or turtles.

MASSACHUSETTS

The Citgo sign, near where the Red Sox play, has been an iconic landmark since 1965. It has 9,000 linear feet of lights!

Boston was founded in 1630 by Puritans, who weren't much fun. For a while, they didn't even allow celebrations like Christmas.

The Fourth of July is also called Independence Day. On July 4, 1776, the Continental Congress signed the Declaration of Independence, marking the birth of our nation.

It might look murky but the river is home to some 20 species of fish, including the alewife and blueback herring, which migrate upriver to spawn. They have to climb fish ladders to get over the dams.

Both the Boston Marathon and the Charles River travel from the suburb of Hopkinton to the city. One takes 26.2 miles and the other takes 80!

Michigan

The Anishinaabe, a group of related indigenous people, have lived here for thousands of years. Historically, they traveled seasonally and used the lakes and rivers as their highways.

The water is sparkling and ultra-clear. Throughout the park, snorkelers and divers explore the many shipwrecks.

On the southeast side of the island lies the wreck of the *Francisco Morazan*. Blinded by snow and fog, the ship ran aground just offshore in 1960.

Thanks to ancient glaciers, this island is covered in sand. Like seaside beaches, there are fun waves to play in on Lake Michigan—but no jellyfish!

CAMP ON SOUTH MANITOU ISLAND

Have you ever been in a time machine? The ferry from Leland, Michigan to South Manitou Island only travels sixteen miles but it's like a passage back in time. Part of Sleeping Bear Dunes National Lakeshore, this island has no cars, few roads, and not a single grocery store. Walk through the woodsy wilderness and imagine what it was like to hunt or fish as an Indigenous American thousands of years ago. Or explore a ghost town and picture life as a European-American logger or farmer in the 1800s. As darkness falls, stake your tent and collect driftwood for a toasty campfire. Don't forget to look up—stars and planets sprinkle the sky!

A coyote is stalking in the wilderness! How did she get out here? She probably got curious and walked over the ice in the wintertime.

Millipedes love the island's moist, ancient cedar forests and like to snack on rotting plants. They have hundreds of wiggly legs.

The island's lighthouse was commissioned in 1871. Climb 117 winding spiral steps to get to the top for an astonishing view.

Beware of chipmunks! While camping, hang your food from a line or keep it in a hard container to avoid these small but feisty mammals.

A rotund little bird zips along the lakeshore, stops, and pulls an insect from the wet sand. Piping plovers are endangered but find a safe home here.

In the Valley of the Giants, cedar trees as old as 500 years stand tall. In the lush ferns, stop to feel the peaceful quietude among these ancient organisms.

After dark, take a peek outside of your cozy lodge. You might get lucky and see the northern lights dancing across the sky.

"Gee!" or "Haw!" is what you say when you want to go right or left. "Whoa!" means stop.

The Boundary Waters Canoe Area Wilderness sprawls over more than a million acres of land and water with no roads or buildings anywhere.

Indigenous people in modern-day Canada, Alaska, and Siberia have traveled by dogsled for centuries. They've used different breeds, including Canadian Inuit dogs, Alaskan huskies, Malamutes, and Samoyeds.

The Ojibwe were the original human inhabitants of this land. They keep many of their traditions alive, such as harvesting wild rice and making birch-bark canoes.

A litter of puppies is born in the spring. They're only a pound or two but grow to nearly 70 pounds by eight months of age, when their instinct to pull kicks in.

MINNESOTA

A flash of fur and tufted ears whizzes by. It's a lynx, which has big paws like snowshoes that help it navigate deep snow.

Canadian Inuit dogs are one of the oldest breeds of domesticated canines on the planet. They love to be petted and played with.

Sled dogs are pack animals, which means they howl, wrestle, and play together. They also vie to be the top dog in the hierarchy.

DOGSLED THE BOUNDARY WATERS

Barks and yelps fill the air as you step onto your dogsled on a crisp winter day. "Hike!" you yell, the command for "go." Release your foot from the brake, and you're off with a jerk into the vast white wilderness of the Boundary Waters! As the dogs run along, you speed across frozen lakes and through boreal forests all frosted with snow. The landscape is quiet and peaceful but lots of wildlife lives here too, including thousands of timber wolves, which are close cousins of your dog team. Look for their tracks, a kill site where they munched on a deer or a moose, or a bedding area where they lay down to rest for the night.

Otters are very playful. In the winter, they make snow slides and shoot into river rapids to hunt for their meals—and also maybe just to have fun!

MISSISSIPPI

Indigenous Americans, including the Choctaw, Chickasaw, and Natchez, have traveled the Natchez Trace corridor for centuries.

Few trees can survive in a watery swamp, but tupelo and bald cypress can. Cypress trees have roots called "knees" that poke out of the water. They help stabilize the plant.

Wildlife love cypress swamps. See if you can spot one of the many snakes, amphibians, or birds.

A nine-banded armadillo is on the move. These mammals have armor-like plates that protect them from predators. They sleep up to 16 hours a day.

Ever heard of quick mud? It's like quicksand but mucky! You generally won't get stuck unless you go off trail.

A bright blue bird zooms by! It's a male indigo bunting. They sing lots of cheerful, high-pitched songs—as many as 200 per hour.

ROAD TRIP THE NATCHEZ TRACE

Buckle your seatbelt, you're going on an adventure on the Natchez Trace Parkway! Around every bend of this curvy, scenic highway is a new surprise: Deer graze by the roadside, turkeys *cluck cluck* in the undergrowth, and hawks circle overhead. Stop to hike the Potkopinu Trail, where centuries of footprints from early Americans created ruts so deep your head is below the tree roots. Drink in the scents of leafy forests draped with Spanish moss like streamers. Explore the site of an ancient Chickasaw village and skip along a boardwalk through a cypress and tupelo swamp. Keep a lookout for alligators sunning on a log!

The whole parkway stretches for a whopping 444 miles and visits three states: Mississippi, Alabama, and Tennessee. The majority is in Mississippi.

In the last two centuries, European settlers and "Kaintucks," workers from the Ohio River region, also used the Natchez Trace. Even President Andrew Jackson walked here during the War of 1812.

Amphibians abound! They're easier to hear than to spot. Sit still for a moment and listen for the symphony of bullfrogs, spring peepers, and cricket frogs.

In fall, cruise through forests tinted gold, burnt sienna, and umber, and fields of cotton that look like snow.

The cave's temperature hovers around 57 degrees and stays the same year-round. Don't forget some layers, even in summer.

In the winter, bats go into a state of hibernation-like torpor. Their metabolism almost stops and their heart rate drops to as slow as four beats per minute.

The Osage Nation, the descendants of the original residents of this area, consider Onondaga Cave to be sacred.

It's important not to touch any formations—the oils and dirt on your fingers can stop them from growing!

Fun fact: In the 1800s, breweries in St. Louis needed a cool place to chill their beer. By 1860, they were using as many as 40 caves as beer storage facilities.

Travelers first started to flock to Onondaga Cave more than 100 years ago during the St. Louis World's Fair in 1904.

Missouri has more than 7,400 caves. That's why it's called the Cave State.

MISSOURI

EXPLORE A DEEP, DARK CAVE

Embrace your inner vampire as you travel deep underground into a hidden wilderness bathed in darkness. Welcome to Onondaga Cave, a wonderland of watery passageways made out of stone. Listen to the drip drip of water. Your whispers echo as you walk through narrow hallways and a giant chamber as long as a football field. Everywhere you look, mysterious formations (known as speleothems) decorate the cavern. Stalactites hang down from the ceiling like streamers. Stalagmites rear up out of the floor like giant stone candles. There are even formations that are wavy and striped like bacon, and discs that look like eggs and pancakes!

Speleothems form as water moves or sits in the cave, depositing minerals like calcite or aragonite over many years. Some can get huge, like the Twins, two stalagmites that tower over 14 feet.

Creepy critters scuttle about. Look for millipedes, centipedes, amphipods (which look like little shrimp), and isopods, which are roly-poly crustaceans.

The unique grotto salamander is a troglobite, which means it lives only in the complete darkness of caves. It is blind and has lost its skin pigment, making it almost translucent.

Montana

On a lazy afternoon, take a break to fly fish for big trout in a meandering river.

As the sun sets, deer and elk peacefully graze in the meadows. See how many points you can count on an elk's antlers.

Roping is more than looping a rope round an animal. Learn how to position your horse and keep the cattle calm as you move among them.

At the end of the day, head to the barn to unsaddle and brush your horse. Then you can offer treats like cookies and carrots.

Horses have personalities just like us. Find a horse that matches your personality, whether you want to ride leisurely in back or lead the team.

Long before European Americans arrived, Indigenous Americans lived on the land now known as Montana. Many tribal nations, such as the Blackfeet, Chippewa Cree, and Crow, still do.

RIDE WITH COWHANDS

There's no freedom quite like trotting through the wild open frontier on horseback. On your trusty steed, do as the cowhands do. With snowy peaks as your backdrop, learn how to rope calves, round up cattle, fix a fence, and gallop through the sagebrush rangeland on a working dude ranch. Ranchers have been raising cows in Montana for well over a century. Listen to the *clop-clop* of your fellow riders, feel the sun on your face, and sniff the scent of sage on the breeze. After a long day in the saddle, you're sure to be hungry. Keep an ear out for the dinner bell!

Ratified in 1862, the Homestead Act allowed any adult citizen of the United States to claim 160 acres of government land. If the person cultivated the land and built a home, it was deemed theirs after five years. This act sped up the settling of the West.

Did you know that cattle have four digestive compartments? They regurgitate and chew their "cud" up to eight hours a day.

West-moving pioneers started ranching cattle in Montana around the 1800s. Cows are docile and easy to take care of, and the settlers raised them for a source of meat and protein.

All across the meadows splash the prettiest wildflowers you've ever seen—Indian paintbrush, purple asters, and cheerful white daisies.

SEE THE SANDHILL CRANE MIGRATION

Visit the Platte River Valley at just the right time in spring and you'll see the whole sky come alive with an incredible swirl of thousands of squawking birds—so many they block out the sun! More than one million sandhill cranes gather on this river to rest and gulp down food on their journey north. Along with geese, ducks, and other species, this is one of the greatest wildlife migrations in North America. Cranes are a talkative species—listen to the clamor of thousands of creatures all chattering at once. Some hop and flap their wings as part of their mating dance. If you have really keen eyes, you might spot one of their cousins, the very rare whooping crane.

Bald eagles follow the cranes. They often eat fish but will also snack on sick, injured, or young cranes too.

While resting in the Platte River Valley, cranes gain as much as 20 percent of their body weight.

Although they look gangly when they have their feet out to land, cranes are graceful fliers. They reach speeds of nearly 50 miles per hour.

Whooping cranes stand more than five feet tall and are one of the most endangered birds in North America. Some say there are as few as 800 left.

The birds love to eat leftover corn in local farmers' fields.

NEBRASKA

Biologists believe that sandhill cranes have been using this area in the middle of the Great Plains as a stopover for 10 million years.

Sandhill cranes travel between 170 and 450 miles each day during their migration. They cruise between 3,500 and 5,000 feet above the surface of Earth.

A male crane is called a roan, a female is called a mare, and a young one is called a colt.

Part of the reason why birds love south-central Nebraska is because of its wet meadows. These shallow areas warm quickly, and the birds find lots of creepy crawlies, plants, and seeds to eat.

To avoid disturbing the birds, sit in a "blind," which is a hut or hiding place where the cranes can't see you.

STARGAZE UNDER A DARK NIGHT SKY

In the middle of the desert in eastern Nevada, a very special place called Great Basin National Park has some of the deepest, darkest nights in the whole country. Here, you can still see what the night might have looked like before humans invented electricity. Turn off your flashlight and look up —the inky sky blazes with a gazillion stars. With your naked eye, discover a vast cosmos filled with stars, planets, and the satiny ribbon of the Milky Way, our very own galaxy. Satellites sail and meteors hurtle across the sky. It's easy to feel blissfully small looking up at our beautiful universe!

Eastern Nevada has such a dark night sky because it's far from light pollution and has little air pollution. Mostly cloudless nights make for prime stargazing.

Darkness is good for the health of all animals, including humans. Light pollution can hamper animals' ability to sleep, travel, hunt, hide, and reproduce.

Rangers sometimes host astronomy programs on Nevada Northern Railway's Star Train. It leaves Ely, Nevada at sunset and chugs into the dark desert west of the park.

Gnarly, twisted bristlecone pine trees are the oldest single living organisms on Earth. They can live for more than 5,000 years.

Because the air is very dry in the desert, the temperature drops quickly. Even in summer, you'll want to bring some toasty layers for your stargazing adventure.

Nevada

Whoosh! There goes one of Great Basin's flying friends. Bats live in caves and come out in the evening to gobble up insects, including mosquitoes.

Want to help get rid of light pollution? Make sure your home has dim outdoor lights that point downward, not up into space. Close blinds in the evening. You could even ask your school if they have dark-sky-friendly lighting.

Don't forget your red flashlight! White lights can mess up your night vision, but the low-light receptors in human eyes are less sensitive to red light.

On a night hike, shine your flashlight on the ground to see tiny glittering eyes like dewdrops. It's a furry little jumping spider, which leaps to catch its prey.

In the evening, the park's "dark" rangers reveal the mysteries of outer space through telescopes. See Saturn's rings, star clusters, and even a nebula, a huge cloud of dust and gas.

At the Lakes of the Clouds Hut, which is only reachable on foot, tuckered hikers warm up, slurp down soup, and hit the hay in bunks.

Cairns are big piles of rocks that help hikers find their way, especially when it's foggy.

Instead of huffing to the top, some people opt to take the Mt. Washington Auto Road or the historic cog railway.

In June, flowers light up the alpine areas. Look for Lapland rosebay, diapensia, and alpine azalea.

New Hampshire

With every 1,000 feet of elevation gain, the temperature drops five degrees. If it's 70 degrees at the bottom, it could be 50 on the summit.

American pipits bob their heads as they strut along the bare tundra looking for insects.

CLIMB ABOVE CLOUDS

Congratulations, you've made it to the top of famous Mt. Washington, the tallest peak in the whole northeast! Because of its height (6,288 feet), it's a magnet for ferocious weather. But today, the skies are clear and you can see as far as Canada and the Atlantic Ocean. You can even see wispy clouds passing by below you. It's no cinch getting up here on the four-mile Tuckerman Ravine Trail. Hikers wind through forests, zigzag up a headwall, and climb like mountain goats over jumbled boulders. But on top, you can slurp down a drink in the cafeteria and even send a postcard from the region's loftiest post office!

In the alpine tundra, plants grow close to the ground because the wind is fierce. The stunted trees are known as krummholz.

A few small mammal species live above the treeline. Spot a mouse, vole, red fox, or ermine, a type of weasel that turns white in winter.

Two butterfly species live here, the White Mountain fritillary and the White Mountain Arctic, which looks just like lichen. They live nowhere else in the world.

CRUISE THE ATLANTIC CITY BOARDWALK

On a sweltering summer day, cool off in the breeze by speeding along on two wheels on the famous Atlantic City boardwalk. Crowds of visitors are enjoying the sun and waves. Cruise by people spiking volleyballs in the sand, surfing the waves, and swimming in the shallows. Stop to play on the gigantic beach, look for crabs, and chase seagulls. Or pedal along to see how many giant casinos you can count along the boardwalk. East coasters have been coming here for their vacations for more than 150 years. In times gone by, strolling lovers in the latest fashions and some of the world's biggest stars, from Marilyn Monroe to the Beatles, trod the boards. Is it time for ice cream yet?

CASINO

How tall do you think those huge beachside hotels are? The tallest one is more than 700 feet high!

Pizza

James Original Salt Water Taffy
& HOME MADE FUDGE

Atlantic City has the oldest beach boardwalk in the world. Construction began in 1870 as a way to keep sand off hotel carpets.

Creamy salt water taffy was first created in Atlantic City in the 1880s. You can still buy it in stores along the boardwalk today.

Long before Atlantic City was founded, these dunes and beaches were the home of the Lenni-Lenape people. They were known as both diplomats and warriors. Their descendants still live in the region today.

Did you know that all of the street names in the original Monopoly board game are named after real places in Atlantic City?

Seagulls caw and swoop overhead, looking for a treat. Watch out—they might steal your hot dog if you're not looking!

TROPICANA
CASINO

Tattoos ~

The boardwalk was originally made of southern pine and Douglas fir. Now, it's made of a very hard Brazilian wood to hold up to all the traffic.

Inline skating might be a thing of the past but every so often you might see a skater twirling over the boards!

Millions of people walk on the boardwalk, which is why all of the boards have to be replaced at least once every 12 years.

NEW JERSEY

NEW MEXICO

To get some speed on your sled, wax the bottom. It can also help to get a running start.

What's that bird crossing the road? A roadrunner, of course! These common desert birds run up to 15 miles per hour.

Be sure to avoid hitting plants, like the spiky soaptree yucca. Indigenous Americans used this plant for lots of things —ropes, sandals, cloth, soap, and food.

When the Merriam's kangaroo rat is scared, it can leap ten feet into the air. That's the equivalent of a kid leaping as high as a skyscraper!

Gypsum is a mineral that is found all over the world and in many household products, including toothpaste.

SLED DOWN GIANT SAND DUNES

In White Sands National Park, the sand is similar to snow, which means you can sled down it! Grab a flying saucer, climb up the steepest dune you can find, and careen down to the bottom. Don't forget to take a look around too—this is the largest gypsum sand dune field in the world, stretching 275 square miles. This land might look vast, dry, and barren but there's lots of life. Over thousands of years, many of the animals have adapted to the environment by becoming white. They might be shy, but look for white moths, white crickets, white mice, and white lizards.

The dunes are very quiet. If you stop talking for a moment, you can listen to the silence.

The desert is almost always sunny—remember your hat, sunscreen, and plenty of water. At night, the temperature plummets when the sun sets.

Little desert cottontails hop about the desert scrub looking for grasses and leaves to eat. They love to come out at dawn and dusk.

Like snow, sand is a great record of animal activity. Look for the tracks of rodents, lizards, and snakes, especially in the morning.

White Sands is part of the Chihuahuan Desert, the largest desert on the continent.

NEW YORK

Peer into a small hole in a building and you might see an American kestrel. These small, spotted falcons are about the size of a dove and like to nest in cavities.

For the best chance at seeing a lot of birds, be silent like a ninja and wear drab colors so you're well camouflaged.

On the big avenues, most people are looking down or straight ahead. Look up and you might spot hawks, vultures, or even an eagle.

A good way to help animals in New York is to prevent littering. Animals can get caught up in plastic bags, string, and other trash.

Just like us, wildlife thrives on a healthy diet. Make sure not to feed animals any human food so they can dine on natural fare.

Believe it or not, New York City has the most diversity of bird species of any county in the state.

Whoosh! New York has one of the highest concentrations of urban peregrine falcons in the world. They dive at 200 miles per hour and like to munch on pigeons.

Squirrels scurry between trees. They are attuned to the sounds of birds, which alert them to nearby predators like hawks.

Coyotes are canids, which means they're related to both dogs and wolves. They adapt to an astonishing range of habitats, from mountains and deserts to the biggest city in the U.S.

Pigeons get a bad rap but they are actually incredibly intelligent. They can learn to recognize words and have even been trained to detect cancer in mammograms.

GO ON AN URBAN WILDLIFE SAFARI

Central Park might be right smack in the middle of New York, the most populous city in America, but it's also a secret wonderland for wildlife. Get out your binoculars and set off in spring or fall to discover some of the 355 bird species that zoom through the city on their annual migrations. Hermit thrushes bounce along the ground looking for insects, and warblers and orioles flit by in flashes of bright colors. Squirrels and chipmunks scamper about the grass and at dusk and dawn, a rare coyote slinks about looking for his next meal.

Don't forget your gloves—there's lots of sharp metal on the boat. And a dive light is a good idea for peering inside the eerie wreck!

Check out the conning tower, the small watertight room on the top of the submarine where sailors used periscopes and directed the boat.

The powerful Gulf Stream current brings warm water up from the south, which is why the water is a delightful 80 degrees in summer.

Brrrrp brrrrp. That's the sound of a funny looking oyster toadfish. The sea is hardly silent. It's full of crackles, pops, and thumps.

NORTH CAROLINA

A sand tiger shark snakes by. It has vicious-looking teeth sticking out in all directions, but don't worry, it has a pretty laid-back attitude.

In the summer, the water is so clear you can sometimes see 100 feet through the light blue sea.

Scuba diving requires a certification, but it allows you to go much deeper than you could if you were snorkeling. The U-352 sits in about 100 feet of water.

SCUBA DIVE A HISTORIC SHIPWRECK

As you descend below the surface of the sea with your SCUBA gear, the spooky outline of a deep, dark shipwreck looms into view. It's the U-352, a German submarine from World War II! As you swim up and down the wreck, look for cool features such as the diving plains that made the boat go up and down, and the galley hatch, one of the submarine's escape doors. You can even see where the Germans loaded torpedoes. After the U-boat sank, algae, corals, and anemones grew on its hull, which is why it's now like a reef. Tons of amberjacks and baitfish swirl about —so many they look like confetti!

North Carolina's coast isn't nicknamed the "Graveyard of the Atlantic" for nothing. More than 1,000 ships, submarines, sailboats, and other vessels met their ends in these shallow waters.

Fifteen sailors lost their lives when this U-boat sank. Thirty-three were rescued and taken as prisoners of war.

This area also has another nickname: Torpedo Alley. During World War II, German U-boats torpedoed merchant ships as they ferried supplies to England.

MOUNTAIN BIKE THE MAAH DAAH HEY TRAIL

The otherworldly striped Badlands of North Dakota are whizzing by as you pedal like a champion on your mountain bike. Cruise down hillsides, splash through creeks, and speed through wide-open grasslands. This is the famous Maah Daah Hey Trail, which winds 144 miles through glorious western North Dakota. In this wild corner of the state, you'll feel like a true explorer as you discover lands full of deer, elk, bighorn sheep, songbirds, and eagles. Overhead, the skies are huge, just like when President Theodore Roosevelt ventured through. On a rest stop, walk just a little ways off the trail and you might find petrified wood or plant fossils!

Rocky pillars, hoodoos, and table rocks decorate the Badlands. Why the scary name? Indigenous Americans like the Lakota Sioux as well as European-American homesteaders called them bad because they're so difficult to travel through.

Pronghorn antelope are not actually a type of antelope. Their closest living relatives are giraffes.

Don't love mountain biking? Try horseback riding or hiking. Many people also backpack the whole trail, camping along the way.

Listen carefully . . . In spring, turkeys gobble as part of their mating practice. In fall, that eerie screaming and whining is a male elk bugling. And many mornings and evenings, coyotes bark and howl.

Remember to shift your weight forward on your bike to climb hills. Shift your weight back on the descents to avoid tumbling over the handlebars.

In the language of the Mandan, Maah Daah Hey loosely means "grandfather" or "an area that has been or will be around for a long time."

Zoom! There goes a prairie falcon flying fast and low over the grass. It's looking for dinner —maybe a bird, rabbit, or lizard.

Mountain bikes have tough frames, big knobby tires, and suspension that help you magically roll over all sorts of rocks and roots.

Trail markers are decorated with a turtle. For the Lakota Sioux, the turtle represents patience, determination, and longevity.

Roll up your pants! The trail crosses the Little Missouri River twice. Make sure the water isn't too high before wading in.

NORTH DAKOTA

A flock of little gray birds flutters by. These dark-eyed juncos hop around on the snowy ground to forage for seeds and bugs.

It's chilly out here! Bring a little heater to warm up your shanty and a thermos of hot chocolate for those frosty winter days.

Groans, pops, and squeaks waft across the lake. It can sound a little eerie, but it's just ice forming deep in the lake.

Where are all the fish? Start with a hole close to shore then move outward if they're not biting. Or simply go where the shanties are clustered.

You'll need some bait for your hook. Wax worms will do the trick. And don't forget a bucket to bring home your fish.

OHIO

A huge white bird with yellow eyes skims the ground looking for prey. Snowy owls nest in the high Arctic in summer but sometimes visit the northern U.S. in winter.

The clearer the ice, the more pure it is. And the purer it is, the stronger it is. Sometimes you can see all the way down to the bottom of the lake.

When it gets really cold and the ice freezes to at least 15 inches, ice fishers will drive out onto the lake in trucks.

Someone small and furry is also fishing near shore. It's a mink, a tough weasel that dives into the icy water looking for fish and frogs to eat.

Often the water is warmest near the bottom of the lake, so drop those lures down deep where the fish are hanging out.

FISH A FROZEN LAKE

What do you get when you combine winter, a frozen lake, and a passion for fishing? Ice fishing! Fish don't hibernate in the wintertime—and neither do anglers. On a chilly winter day, venture out onto the ice (make sure it's at least four inches thick) and drill a hole with your auger. In a little tent or ice shanty, drop your line into the hole and bounce it up and down to catch a sleepy fish's attention. Feel a tug? Reel it in to see if it's a bluegill, perch, or crappie. You can either let it go or take it home for dinner.

Oklahoma

Millions of years ago, an inland sea deposited layers of salt here. Over time, soil covered the salt, then groundwater percolated up through the sand and evaporated, leaving a crust. Crystals form from salty water mixing with gypsum.

DIG FOR CRYSTALS

Dig in the sand here at Salt Plains National Wildlife Refuge and you will almost surely find treasure! Selenite crystals hide just under the surface of the sand and grow in beautiful hourglass shapes and clusters that weigh up to 38 pounds. In the vast white salt flats, dig a hole a few inches to a foot deep. Splash some water into the pit and wash the sand and clay from the sides. Feel around gently to see if you can find crystals sticking out of the earth. Some people find enough crystals to load up a whole bucket!

Why do these crystals have a fetching reddish brown color? It's because of the iron oxide in the soil.

DIG AREA

No Vehicles Beyond This Point

You're likely to find crystals that, along with sediments, form an hourglass shape. No other selenite crystals in the world feature this hourglass shape.

The crystals you find here are made of selenite, a crystallized form of gypsum, which is a common mineral.

With few plants, this place looks like the moon. But amazingly, tens of thousands of shorebirds gather on their annual migrations.

The nation's tallest birds, whooping cranes, visit this refuge every fall and spring. They are highly endangered but their numbers are growing!

You'll need a shovel, a bucket of water to splash in your hole, and patience so you can unearth your fragile crystals without breaking them.

It takes about seven years for crystals to form. Refuge managers rotate the areas where visitors are allowed to dig so there's plenty of time for new crystals to grow.

Jackpot! You found all sorts of crystal types: single ones, twins, and even clusters.

Snowy plovers breed on the salt flats where they make nests out of stones and invertebrate skeletons. They like to eat salt brine flies. They are sensitive creatures, so it's important not to scare or disturb them.

For thousands of years, Plains Indians and Osage traveled to the salt flats to gather salt, tan hides, and salt their meat.

Need a tasty flavoring? Wild ginger tastes like regular ginger but it's smaller than the kind you find in a grocery store. Their rhizomes are slimmer than a pencil.

"What is a weed?" asked author Ralph Waldo Emerson. "A plant whose virtues have not yet been discovered."

Remember the golden rule of foraging: Only eat plants that you are 100 percent sure you can identify! Learning from an expert is a great idea.

Let your taste buds lead the way. Even the same plant species can taste very different depending on where it's growing.

What's for dessert? Pick some thimbleberries, salmonberries, or huckleberries right off the bushes!

OREGON

SURVIVE IN THE WILD

In Oregon, a secret world of delicious free food is hiding right under your nose, you just have to know where to look. Foraging is like a treasure hunt. Venture off into the wild (or even your own backyard) with keen eyes to collect a feast of plants. In spring, pluck tender greens like chickweed and dandelion. Throughout the warm months, mushrooms sprout and berries grow by the bushel. And in fall, white acorns and beaked hazelnuts fall from the trees. Whatever you find, bring it all to your campsite, light a fire, and whip up dishes like morel mushroom soup, wildflower salad, and acorn pudding!

To ensure there's enough food for next year, make sure not to fully uproot plants unless there's a huge abundance of them in one area, like more than 20.

Parts of western Oregon were among the most populated areas of the continent before Europeans arrived. That's because they were so abundant with wild food.

Every plant goes through a life cycle, from germinating and growing to its reproductive phase, when it sprouts flowers and seeds. A plant can taste really different depending on its phase of life.

The best way to get tons of nutrients is not just to eat wild plants but to eat lots of different kinds of plants, like our ancestors did.

WHOOSH DOWN A NATURAL WATERSLIDE

On a hot summer day, step into Meadow Run, sit down, and get ready for a wild ride! Over thousands of years, this stream carved a slick chute into the rock here at Ohiopyle State Park, which is full of creeks, waterfalls, and vibrant forests. Now, the stone funnel is a rollicking all-natural waterslide. Hold on as you hurtle right, left, and down into little hollows, like an amusement park ride. At the end, the powerful water shoots you into a big shallow pool. Catch your breath before clambering up the rocks to try it again!

In summer, the blooms of rhododendrons and azaleas decorate the banks of the river.

Count yourself lucky if you see a fisher, a secretive weasel with retractable claws. Fishers are one of the few predators known to dine on porcupines.

Don't fancy swimming? Take a hike on a trail next to Meadow Run or grab your fishing rod to see if you can catch some trout.

Something is slithering beneath your feet! It's a hellbender, an aquatic salamander that can grow as long as two-and-a-half feet. When it feels threatened, it produces a snot-like slime.

Pennsylvania

A flicker of red lights up the trees. It's a northern cardinal with its incredible crimson plumage and head crest.

What do you get when you combine lots of cliffs and lots of water? Waterfalls! In addition to the slides, this park has many comely cascades.

Water is very powerful. A smart slider assesses the water before hopping in. A mellower cascade, Otter Slides, lies upstream of the bigger waterslide.

The river runs over 300-million-year-old Homewood sandstone, which also contains plant fossils. Look on the edges of the riverbed for these hidden treasures.

This gorge is much warmer than the surrounding areas because of its steep walls, which trap warm air, and the temperate Youghiogheny River that flows through.

Take care! The rocks are very slippery. Make sure you bring good shoes and walk carefully.

Over the past 50 years, the water temperature in the bay has risen 3 degrees because of climate change. That means that species are changing too—there are more lobsters and fewer blue crabs.

In sailor speak, the right side of a boat is called starboard, the left side is called port. The bow is the front and the stern is the back.

To sail into the wind, you'll have to learn how to zigzag. A tack is a turn into the wind and a jibe is a turn when you're following the wind.

Mute swans are floating in the brackish water. They were originally brought in from Europe but now there are so many they crowd out native birds.

It looks like fish are boiling out of the sea. It might be because bluefish or scup are chasing a school of smaller fish.

RHODE ISLAND

Before English settlers arrived in what is now Newport, native people had been living on Aquidneck Island for more than 5,000 years.

Big, fancy houses dot the shoreline. Newport was a playground for the rich and famous during the Gilded Age.

Narragansett Bay was carved out by glaciers, and Newport has one of the deepest natural harbors on the eastern seaboard. It gets about 24 feet deep.

You may not get your driver's license until you're a teenager but there are no rules against young kids sailing in their own boats!

It's rare for a boat to capsize but if it happens, remember this very important rule: Always stay with your boat!

SAIL THE SHINY SEA

Breathe in the salt air as you head out in a sailboat to explore the open sea! In your very own craft, steer downwind, exploring the islands and hidden coves of Narragansett Bay. Newport, Rhode Island is famous for its calm water and steady breeze, which fills your sails and sends you cruising along. Listen to the lapping of the water on your hull and the flapping sails as you learn to understand the signals of the ocean. Pretty soon you'll be reading the wind and discovering new and distant shorelines full of cool new sights, smells, and sounds!

In 1861, the Union Army took over Hilton Head, causing the white plantation owners to flee. Formerly enslaved people then started arriving and established Mitchelville in 1862.

About 3,000 people lived in Mitchelville in the late 1800s. Even Harriet Tubman, the famous conductor on the Underground Railroad, visited.

The Gullah-Geechee (two terms for the same people) descended from many different African tribes and together created a unique language, cuisine, and spiritual tradition. Today, they also live in North Carolina, Georgia, and Florida.

STEP BACK IN TIME

Visiting the historic town of Mitchelville on Hilton Head Island is like a time-traveling adventure. Founded during the Civil War, Mitchelville was the first self-governed town of freed Africans in the nation. Under the bright South Carolina sun, run around stands of huge live oaks to discover replicas of an old general store, a church, and a homestead from the 1860s. Nearby, the residents enjoyed access to a bird-filled marsh and a wide beach. Imagine what it would have been like to own your own land and start your own business after escaping the horrors of slavery. Today, the Gullah, the descendants of West Africans enslaved in America, still live on Hilton Head and can spin tales about their amazing families.

Long-beaked whimbrels are running across the sand at breakneck speed. These birds were once mercilessly hunted in the 19th century but their populations have partly recovered.

SOUTH CAROLINA

A flock of brown pelicans soars in the distance. To hunt fish, they plunge headlong into the water at speed.

A ring shout is a ceremony that Gullah people hold when they have something to celebrate or something to mourn. Women and men dance in a circle, clap, and chant together.

Without any assistance from the government, the people of Mitchelville built 500 homes, stores, churches, and schools and made their own system of law.

On the big wide stretch of sand, look for huge horseshoe crabs. If you see a shell, pick it up— a hermit crab might live inside!

The salt marsh next to Mitchelville is like an all-you-can-eat buffet for shorebirds. Look for egrets and herons as they wade for food.

Head to the nearby beach to build sand castles and play in the waves. Back in the 1800s, Mitchelville residents raced horses along the beaches.

Between 30 and 37 million years ago, alligators, oreodonts, and five-foot-tall pig-like creatures lived in the region, which was covered in muggy forests. Now only their fossils remain.

Why are the Badlands so colorful and weirdly shaped? Layers of sedimentary rock formed one on top of the other over millions of years. Then about 500,000 years ago, erosion from rainfall started to wear them away into strange forms.

Animals big and small live in the Badlands. Look for bighorn sheep, bison, skunks, and frogs.

Between 67 and 75 million years ago, the area was an inland sea. Imagine 60-foot marine reptiles and turtles the size of cars.

In the national park, collecting fossils is illegal. But you may collect some in the national forests or on private land if you have permission from the landowner.

South Dakota

The Badlands have all sorts of wacky wonders. See if you can find windows in the cliffs or wormhole sandstone, which looks like Swiss cheese.

Humans have inhabited this area for at least 12,000 years. Currently, the Lakota live here.

This is one of the largest remaining tracts of mixed-grass prairie. More than 400 species of plants live here.

In the evening, shiny eyes stare out at you from the darkness—black-footed ferrets! These nocturnal mammals live in underground burrows and eat lots of prairie dogs.

Black-footed ferrets were once thought to be extinct but a Wyoming sheepdog stumbled upon a small population in 1981. The animals were bred and reintroduced to the wild but are still very endangered.

SEARCH FOR FOSSILS

In 2010, a seven-year-old girl was visiting Badlands National Park with her family when she discovered the fossil of a lifetime. Partly buried in a butte not far from the visitor's center, she found a rare nimravid skull. What's a nimravid? A big cat-like creature with teeth like swords! You too can discover treasures in the Badlands, where erosion is turning up new fossils all the time. Hike through these colorful striped hoodoos and buttes—you never know, you might see a piece of an ancient camel, three-toed horse, or rhinoceros. If you spot anything interesting, leave it in place, take a picture, and tell a ranger, who might get started on a real dig!

TENNESSEE

WATCH A FABULOUS FIREFLY LIGHT SHOW

In late spring, a mysterious phenomenon unfolds in the Great Smoky Mountains. After dark, thousands of fireflies, or lightning bugs, all flash at the exact same time, brightening the whole forest. People come from near and far to see this natural light show, which only lasts for a few weeks. Watch as the male beetles gleam six to eight times then rest for about eight seconds before repeating the pattern. The light flashes are part of the insects' mating ritual—they use their lamps to help find each other. (The females sit on the ground and respond with a faint light.) Lots of other lightning bugs dot the mountains but the synchronous fireflies are the only ones that all flash together.

Hear that eerie whinnying and trilling? That's the eastern screech owl, which sleeps all day and hunts insects and rodents by night.

There are many species of fireflies and each one has its own pattern of flashes. These patterns help them recognize each other.

You'll want a flashlight so you can find your way in the dark. Once you sit down, turn it off so your eyes can adjust—and so you don't blind other visitors!

Most fireflies emit a greenish-yellow light but one type shines bluish. They're called blue ghosts.

When a living being can emit light from its body, it's called bioluminescence. Certain types of jellyfish, plankton, fungus, snails, and worms can all make light.

How does bioluminescence work? It involves chemical reactions within the organism's body that create particles of light.

Fireflies like warm and moist conditions. If it's really cold, misty, or rainy, the bugs won't be as frisky.

Bobcats prowl about at night but they are tough to spot. About twice as big as a house cat, they have tufted ears and stubby tails.

In this area, lightning bugs take a year to grow out of their larvae stage. They only live as grown-ups for about three weeks.

Many firefly species are declining because of development and light pollution. You can help by dimming lights at night.

TEXAS

A big black bird opens its wings to dry them off. Double-crested cormorants spend a lot of time in the water and dry their wings in the sun.

To learn to kiteboard, sign up for lessons with a real coach! You'll learn to steer by keeping your hands close to the center of the bar and moving the bar very slowly and smoothly back and forth. Avoid flying directly downwind, especially if it's gusty!

A tiny newly hatched turtle is making its way to the sea. South Padre Island is a nesting area for the world's smallest and most endangered sea turtle, the Kemp's Ridley.

KITEBOARD SOUTH PADRE ISLAND

With a huge kite in the air, a strong wind, and a board on your feet, you're speeding across the surface of the ocean like magic. Harnessing the power of the wind, see if you can lift off the surface. You might even try doing tricks like flipping and spinning—it feels like flying! Explore the waters along South Padre Island. When you look north all you can see are beautiful sand dunes. All around, migratory and shore birds fly and dive. In the beautiful clear green water below, you might spot a sea turtle!

Padre Island is the world's longest barrier island. Barrier islands help protect shorelines from storms.

South Padre Island is right on the Central Flyway, a big migration route for birds traveling between South, Central, and North America. How many different bird species can you count?

If you feel like you're going too fast or in the wrong direction, simply let go of the bar or eject the kite from your harness and the kite will fall from the sky.

A fellow mammal has come to frolic with you! Dolphins are playful and like to ride and jump in the waves.

When you have a gigantic kite and very long lines, it's important to practice in places with nothing to hit. The sandy flats and open beaches of South Padre Island are perfect.

Kiteboarding is basically the same thing as kitesurfing and kiting. You can ride on flat water, do tricks, or even launch off of waves.

The southern Gulf Coast has tons of wind all year round, and people come from all over the world to kite and windsurf.

UTAH

Spring and fall are the best times to visit this desert. In summer, temperatures top 100 degrees. In winter, they can dive below zero.

Grand Staircase-Escalante is so rugged and riddled with canyons, it was the last place in the continental United States to be mapped.

Since long before European Americans arrived, Paiutes, Utes, Navajo, and Hopi have lived here. Their ancestors' ancient rock art and granaries remain.

How do slot canyons form? Over thousands of years, water travels through grooves in the sandstone, carving deeper and deeper until the grooves turn into gorges.

CANYONEER A SLOT CANYON

You've probably heard of the Grand Canyon, but have you ever heard of a slot canyon? Instead of being really big and wide, slot canyons are very tall and skinny. The state of Utah claims the largest concentration of slot canyons in the world. Some are extremely steep and require ropes and harnesses so you can rappel into them. For others, you only need a sense of adventure. Try Peek-a-boo and Spooky in Grand Staircase-Escalante National Monument. Get ready to use both your hands and feet to climb up and down these winding sandstone gorges. Sometimes they're so slim, canyoneers have to remove their backpacks to squeeze through.

When exploring slot canyons, you'll use a technique called stemming. Put one foot on one cliff and one foot on the other and shuffle along.

Ringtails are shy raccoon-like mammals that are occasionally seen at dusk and dawn. They can climb vertical cliffs and even cacti!

Not many animals live inside slot canyons but occasionally Mexican spotted owls nest on cliff ledges in remote areas.

As you shimmy and scoot, notice the cool, gritty rock under your hands. Navajo sandstone is about 180 million years old.

To avoid flash floods, which arrive suddenly, keep an eye on the weather. Between July and September, afternoon thunderstorms are common.

In the rocky, sandy land between slot canyons, look for desert spiny lizards and whiptails.

Hooo-wooo-hooo. That sorrowful cry is the sound of a mourning dove. Doves thrive in semi-open areas such as forest clearings and farms.

Long ago, the ancestors of the Western Abenaki people and the Mohicans were the main human residents of the Green Mountains. They lived here for more than 10,000 years. The Western Abenaki still live here today.

A prickly beast is scuttling around in the bushes—it's a North American porcupine, which has 30,000 quills!

The spooky cry of a loon echoes across the pond. Loons love quiet, remote lakes where they can dive for fish without being pestered by noisy humans.

Winters are harsh in the northeast, which means that tender deciduous trees need to shed their leaves. All those fallen leaves decompose on the forest floor, making yummy food and homes for organisms that live in the soil.

Different species of trees turn different colors. Sugar maples turn orange-red, oaks turn red, rust or bronze, and birches and aspens turn brilliant shades of yellow.

It's early October, there's a nip in the air, and the forests of Vermont are ablaze with color. It looks as if a clumsy giant spilled a box of red, orange, and yellow paints all over the place. Skip through the cool, dim deciduous woods, breathe in the earthy scent of loam, and jump on all of the crunchy leaves that are falling to the ground. Feeling ambitious? Climb to the top of a mountain to see a colorful quilt of trees or paddle silently on a pond in a canoe. Keep a lookout for diving loons and munching moose.

Chlorophyll helps absorb light so the plant can make energy for photosynthesis. It's also what gives leaves their green color.

Blue jays sure are noisy! Listen to their boisterous calls and look for the bright blue flashes of their plumage.

As the days shorten in fall, plants produce less chlorophyll, which means the green hue fades and their other natural colors come out.

Every year, foliage looks slightly different depending on the temperature and the weather. The best showings usually come after sunny days and crisp evenings.

Vermont

HIKE THE WORLD'S LONGEST TRAIL

Slinking near some of the country's biggest cities, a hidden footpath leads 2,193 miles through woods, meadows, and mountains all the way from Georgia to Maine. It's the longest hiking-only trail in the world. Can you imagine hiking the whole thing? Every year, more than 3,000 people try! But you don't have to hike the entire Appalachian Trail to have a fun time. On a 3.9-mile climb to McAfee Knob, tramp through hardwood forests, hop over streams, and peek inside two shelters. Then discover what some people say is Virginia's best vista. From an outcropping at over 3,000 feet, gaze over giant valleys and mountains like royalty.

Eeeeeeeeeeeye! That's the chilling scream of a red-tailed hawk, one of the most common raptors on the continent.

If you hiked the entire Appalachian Trail, you would climb the same elevation as you would if you summited Mt. Everest 16 times!

Thru-hikers who hike the whole AT are a funny bunch. They carry all of their belongings on their backs and adopt goofy trail names like Rodeo Clown and Pink Monkey.

Virginia has the longest stretch of the Appalachian Trail of any state. It winds more than 500 miles through Virginia alone.

Eastern rat snakes grow up to seven feet long, but don't worry, they're not venomous! When threatened, they emit an icky musky smell.

On sections of the Appalachian Trail, you might see what long-distance hikers call "trail magic," when generous people offer food, rides, or other favors to tuckered-out hikers.

This primo view attracts tons of hikers! As always, make sure you don't leave any trace of trash so people can enjoy a pristine experience after you.

Keep an eye out for rhododendrons and the white flowers of mountain laurel that bloom in early summer.

The tulip poplar grows very tall and straight. Early European-American explorers used it to build cabins. During the Civil War, workers used the wood to build railroads.

VIRGINIA

Tufted puffins nest on cliffs so predators can't reach them. A puffin parent can bring up to 20 fish home to its chicks at one time.

What's the fastest way to get to San Juan Island from Seattle? A float plane! Soar over the shimmering sea in a tiny airplane that lands right on the water.

Is that a fried egg passing by in the water? Nope! It's a fried egg jellyfish, which has yellow organs and a white bell.

SEA KAYAK THE SAN JUAN ISLANDS

On the silky waters of the Salish Sea, glide along in your bright red kayak. Suddenly a gigantic dorsal fin spikes out of the water—a pod of killer whales is passing by! The San Juan Islands are famous for their whales, and orcas are the stars of the show with dorsal fins that can stretch six feet high. Everywhere you look, wildlife swims, floats, flits, and flies. Look for bald eagles nesting on the wooded islands—their heads look like golf balls in the trees. In the bays and inlets, seals and sea lions frolic. Watch as they pop up near your boat and eye you curiously.

Like orcas, Dall's porpoises are black with white patches but they are smaller and have triangle-shaped dorsal fins. They swim up to 34 miles per hour.

After a hot, sunny day, evening brings a magical light show called bioluminescence. Go kayaking at night to see special plankton light up the sea as you paddle through it.

A fishy smell wafts by . . . humpback whale breath! These majestic mammals feed here in fall before migrating to the tropics for the winter.

Underwater, sea lions loop and play. On shore, they laze around on a rocky beach.

Orcas talk to each other in squeaks, shrieks, and other calls. Each family or pod has a distinct dialect, kind of like an accent.

In San Juan County, there are 172 named islands and reefs. That's a lot of shoreline to explore!

WASHINGTON

The New River Gorge Bridge is the longest single arch bridge in the western hemisphere. One day a year in the fall, BASE jumpers leap off of it and float to the ground with parachutes.

These woods are packed with yummy things to eat, from morel and chanterelle mushrooms to wild strawberries you can pluck right from the forest floor.

A mellower stretch of whitewater lies upstream in the Upper New River Gorge, where the river tumbles into Class II and occasionally Class III rapids.

In the Lower New River Gorge, there are more than 25 rapids, from easy Class II to heart-pounding Class V.

West Virginia is a hotbed for salamanders, with more than 30 species. Salamanders have permeable skin and gooey eggs, which means they're sensitive to any pollution in the environment.

The New River carves through the Appalachian Plateau, where the rocks are as old as 330 million years. This river is actually older than the mountains themselves.

RAFT THE RAPIDS IN THE LOWER NEW RIVER GORGE

Feel the butterflies in your stomach as you approach the rolling waves of a whitewater rapid in the Lower New River Gorge. Bouncing up and down and twirling about, you get completely soaked with splashes! When the river calms, see how many colors of green you can pick out in the thick, dripping rainforests on the banks. In this untamed forest, deer, foxes, black bears, opossums, and bobcats roam. In the summer, the river water is 80 degrees and inviting. On a mellow section, slip over the side of your boat like an otter to cool off in one of the oldest rivers in the world.

A bright red bird with black wings flutters between trees. Male scarlet tanagers look totally different from females, which are yellow with greenish wings.

Look straight down into the sparkling clear water. Smallmouth bass, walleye, and catfish swim right beneath your boat.

Banded water snakes swim with their heads above the water. These aquatic snakes like to swallow fish and frogs alive.

The New River Gorge is an important refuge in the battle against climate change. The forests absorb at least 145,000 metric tons of carbon dioxide from the atmosphere every year.

WEST VIRGINIA

A flock of black-capped chickadees sails through the trees. They are often curious about human beings, and they have a complex language of calls.

Every February, more than 13,000 skiers converge on this trail system for the famous American Birkebeiner, the biggest cross-country marathon in the United States.

Riding a bike on snow seems crazy until you have a fat bike, which has humongous tires. Fat bikes roll over just about everything in your path, including crunchy snow. They are only allowed on this trail system once a year during the Fat Bike Birkie.

Kids as young as three years old participate in the races in front of cheering fans with cowbells. After winning a medal, collect your hot cocoa and cookies!

Wisconsin sure is snowy. It can snow as early as September and as late as June.

The American Birkebeiner race and trail system attracts elite athletes from all over the world. See if you can spot an Olympian!

In the middle of winter, the temperature is often in the 20s but it can get as cold as 35 below. Brrr!

Wisconsin

A bald eagle plunges down to a stream. Since 1782, this bird has been the symbol of the United States.

Eight public cabins dot the trail system. Build a fire in a wood-burning stove and enjoy a picnic before turning around and skiing home.

In contrast to classic skiing, skate skiing is more like ice skating. With long skinny skis, you can go really fast.

CROSS-COUNTRY SKI THROUGH SNOWY WOODS

All you can hear is the sound of your breath and the swish of your skis as you speed through the silent north woods of Wisconsin. The famous American Birkebeiner Trail system has over 60 miles of paths that wind through sparkling forests all blanketed in snow. Sometimes the trail is so wide, it's like a superhighway just for skiers. See how fast you can go as you schuss up and down rolling hills, careen around turns, and sail over bridges. Lots of other life lives here too. A deer quietly walks through the woods and a fox steals across the trail right behind you.

GO ON A WILDLIFE SAFARI

Don't forget your binoculars! Grand Teton National Park is packed with wildlife. On the valley floor, you don't even need to leave your car to see bison, deer, and elk grazing on the sagebrush flats. Pronghorn dash and coyotes trot about the valley too. As you hike in the forest, you might spot one of the Tetons' famous grizzly and black bears—but be sure to stay a safe distance away. Bears are protective of their young. Higher up in the woods, look for mountain lion tracks and listen for the eerie howls of a wolf pack. See that flash of red, yellow, and black? That's a western tanager, one of the most colorful birds in the forest.

Before Europeans arrived, the Shoshone, Bannock, Blackfeet, Crow, Flathead, Gros Ventre, Nez Perce, and other tribes gathered and hunted here.

Wolves and bears prey on moose, but moose aren't wimps. They run fast or fight back by kicking with their powerful legs.

The Snake River flows through the valley carrying fish such as cutthroat trout and Utah chub. You might see a moose swimming across!

The forests are full of fir, spruce, aspen, and lodgepole pine. Lodgepoles are adapted to fire. Their cones produce tons of seeds after a scorching.

The sage grouse lives in the valley and is known for its wild mating dance. Males strut, fan their tails, and make popping sounds to catch a mate's eye.

Many of the exciting mammals and birds you see wouldn't exist without insects to eat. Bears slurp up army cutworm moths, ant colonies, and grubs.

WYOMING

The Tetons rise an amazing 7,000 feet from the valley floor. Over 10 million years, earthquakes along the Teton fault built these mountains and depressed the valley.

Hike in groups and make noise to make sure you don't surprise a bear. Most bears wander safely away if they hear you coming.

Pronghorn antelope can run away from predators really quickly, up to 60 miles per hour. They can leap 20 feet at a time.

The calliope hummingbird is the smallest bird in North America and weighs one tenth of an ounce, about as much as a penny!

Did you know that elk have two canine teeth called ivories? Scientists think they are vestiges from evolutionary ancestors that had big tusks.

5 ADVENTURES IN YOUR OWN NEIGHBORHOOD!

A daring spirit can lead you to amazing heights, hidden depths, and lots of other exciting places. But you don't need to go far to have a big, fun adventure. Try out these activities in your own backyard or neighborhood. All you need is curiosity, a little bit of courage, and keen powers of observation. What new things might you see, hear, feel, smell, and learn along the way?

GO ON A CAMPING EXPEDITION— IN YOUR BACKYARD!

What would it be like to sleep in the wild? Start to find out by creating your own shelter in your backyard—or, if you don't have a backyard, the wilds of your own living room! What will you use for your tent poles? What about a tarp? And what kind of device will you use to light your way at night? Gather your supplies and provisions, then try out your shelter to see how it holds up overnight.

SWIM IN A LAKE, POND, RIVER, OR THE SEA

Human beings can't go long without water, which means that settlements of any size always have water nearby. Set forth to find the hidden bodies of water in your neighborhood, whether it's a stream, river, pond, lake, or the ocean. Explore the banks or shores to see what kind of flora and fauna you can find in this hidden watery world. Feeling brave? Dip your toes in—or plunge all the way!

SEATTLE, WA
SEP
· 16 ·
2020
98109

· NEW YORK CITY ·

GET LOST, THEN FIND YOUR WAY HOME

Even in your own neighborhood, there are likely streets, alleys, and other areas you have never explored. With a grown-up, take a bus to a stop (not too far from home) where you have never disembarked—or be dropped off in a car. Then find your way home via a route you have never taken before. Good explorers are sharp observers. What new buildings, trees, plants, animals, and people did you discover on your expedition?

EXPLORE THE NIGHT SKY

By observing the night sky overhead, the ancients were able to adventure around the planet, navigating across continents and oceans. You too can learn the movements of the stars and planets by paying close attention. Even in a big city, you can spot a few stars and the moon on a clear night. Keep a diary of what is happening in the cosmos by observing every evening. In what phase is the moon? When does it rise and set? Where do the brightest stars or constellations appear in the sky and how do they move across it?

HONOLULU, HI
SEP
21
2019
96820

GO ON A WILDLIFE SAFARI

Whether you live in the middle of a city, in the suburbs, or on a farm, wild animals are everywhere! You just have to know where to look. With a notebook in hand, venture into your neighborhood to see how many species you can count. You might spot squirrels and chipmunks dashing between trees or robins bouncing along the grass. Don't forget to look up to see soaring birds, and down to find earthworms and insects.

INDEX

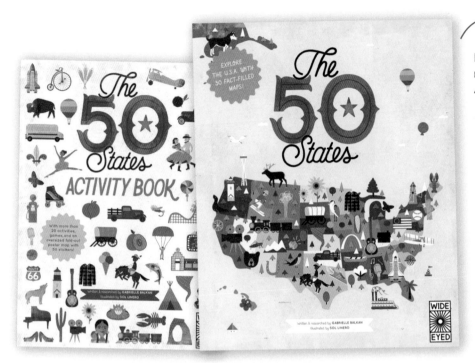

THE 50 STATES

In 51 charmingly illustrated infographic maps, explore every state of the USA from Alabama to Wyoming and the nation's capital, to discover more than 2,000 facts that celebrate the people, cities, nature, and historic events that have helped make America what it is today. Additionally, find an expansive guide to the state flags and US presidents. Each state's map also contains information about which states it neighbors, its bodies of water and borders, as well as where it is situated in the country. Did you know that while Hawaii shares its border with no one, both Missouri and Tennessee border eight other states? Many state parks, battlefields, national forests, and reservations are also included to inspire you to respect and explore the great outdoors.

THE 50 STATES: ACTIVITY BOOK

This companion activity book to **The 50 States** is packed with puzzles, state trivia, picture scrambles, dot-to-dots, and more. At the back, find a double-sided fold-out map and more than 50 stickers. Have fun filling in your own Tall Tale about a trip you made in the U.S.A., then play a Great Race game with a friend. Ponder crosswords and word searches, and test your knowledge with a presidential puzzle, as you try to remember which state historic presidents came from. Finally, let your creative juices flow as you draw your very own, brand new state!

ONLY IN AMERICA

Only in America explores the strangest claims to fame and the most unusual place names every state has to offer. Visit the city of Dinosaur, drop by the Pizza Museum, and find out where it's illegal to feed a pig without a permit in this state-by-state compendium of weird laws, quirks, one-offs, and unusual records only to be found in the wonderfully wacky U.S. of A.

NATIONAL PARKS OF THE U.S.A.

Armchair travelers and budding explorers will love this treasury of America's stunning national parks. Containing illustrated maps and fascinating facts about the flora and fauna unique to each of the 21 parks portrayed, this lushly illustrated coast-to-coast journey documents in large format the nation's most magnificent and sacred places. Divided by region (East, Central, Rocky Mountains, West, Tropics, and Alaska), each park is introduced by a stunning artwork of one of its scenes and a summary of its makeup, followed by individual illustrations of the animals and plants that make their homes there.

NATIONAL PARKS OF THE U.S.A. ACTIVITY BOOK

The perfect companion to **National Parks of the U.S.A.**, this activity book is packed with wildlife and nature facts, park trivia, spotters guides, and a kaleidoscope of activities including coloring, puzzles, and quizzes. Follow the park animals as you find your way through a seemingly never-ending maze, spot the difference between some amazing creepy crawlies, complete a ferocious crossword full of hungry predators, find your feathered park friends in a bird word search, and design your very own national park. Use the spotters guide for each park to see if you can find grunting northern elephant seals, fluttering hummingbirds, bounding snowshoe hares, and lots of other wonderful creatures. At the back, find a fold-out poster and 50 animal stickers.

50 MAPS OF THE WORLD

An essential addition to the bookshelf of any travel-lover, map-maestro or geography genius. Spanning the world from Spain to Singapore, Colombia to Canada, Turkey to Tanzania, discover all you need to know about some of the most awesome places on Earth. Geography, history and culture spill from the pages in this densely-packed treasure-trove of travel knowledge. Each two-page spread is dedicated to a different country, providing both quick-fire facts and the chance to delve deeper into what makes every nation unique. Natural wonders, bustling metropolises, storied pasts and cultural icons are all presented in expert detail to inspire young globetrotters.

Text © 2020 Kate Siber. Illustrations © 2020 Lydia Hill.

First published in 2020 by Wide Eyed Editions, an imprint of The Quarto Group.
First published in paperback in 2024.
100 Cummings Center, Suite 265D, Beverly, MA 01915, USA.
T +1 978-282-9590 **www.Quarto.com**

ISBN 978-0-7112-9187-4
eISBN 978-0-7112-5446-6

The illustrations were created digitally
Set in Vibur and Quicksand

Published by Georgia Amson-Bradshaw
Designed by Myrto Dimitrakoulia
Edited by Georgia Amson-Bradshaw
Edited for paperback by Claire Saunders
Production by Dawn Cameron

Manufactured in Guangdong, China TT012024

9 8 7 6 5 4 3 2 1